Keys to Artistic Performance

4 Early Intermediate to Intermediate Pieces to Inspire Imaginative Performance

Ingrid Jacobson Clarfield
Dennis Alexander

 Color

 Pedaling

 Rubato

 Characterization

 Choreography

We extend our heartfelt appreciation to those who helped us during the various phases of writing this book:
Hearther Atagan, Tom Gerou, E. L. Lancaster, Kristen Watkins, and especially Carol Matz.

This book is dedicated to my beautiful new granddaughter, Elizabeth Faith Newell.
You have brought so much joy to my life.

Special thanks to my dear friend, Dean Elder,
for sharing his insights on all my projects.

—*Ingrid Jacobson Clarfield*

Table of Contents

KEYS TO ARTISTIC PERFORMANCE

The Purpose of This Book

This book is designed to teach students the skills that will transform average performances into polished, artistic ones. These skills are used by professional pianists to make their performances more expressive and dramatic. They are the "keys to artistic performance."

The five "keys" for achieving performance artistry are:

- Color
- Pedaling
- Rubato
- Characterization
- Choreography

These "keys" should be thought about during the learning process and reinforced after the music is technically and rhythmically solid.

Choice of Music and Sequencing

The authors have selected repertoire that showcases the five "keys" highlighted in this series. Several familiar favorites have been included, as well as some less-familiar pieces. Dennis Alexander has composed pieces especially for this series that feature and highlight the "keys to artistic performance."

The pieces are arranged in approximate order of technical and musical difficulty. However, they can be assigned in a different order to support and reinforce the student's technical and musical needs.

Editorial Suggestions

Each piece appears in its original form with editorial suggestions. Fingerings are provided to facilitate musicality and technique. Students should try suggested alternate fingerings and use the ones that are most comfortable.

All of the composers' original indications for dynamics and articulation are provided. However, there are many additional suggestions included to help the student achieve better balance, voicing and greater musical expression.

Metronome markings are suggested in a wide range to allow students to find a tempo at which they can comfortably perform the music artistically.

Once you have learned all the correct notes, rhythms and basic dynamics of the music you are studying, there are certain things you can do to make your performance truly artistic. In this book, you will learn some of the skills that concert pianists use to make their performances more dramatic and imaginative.

How to Use This Book

Information about the "keys to artistic performance" appears on pages 4–10. Special symbols and terminology indicated in the music are listed on pages 8 and 10 for easy reference. In addition, at the top of each page of music there is a section called "Keys to This Piece." These "keys" apply specifically to the piece that follows, and reinforce information found in the more general *Keys to Artistic Performance* section.

You may also incorporate your own ideas to help make your performance even more interesting. The more expressive and dynamic your performance is, the more you and your audience will enjoy it!

Most people relate color to paintings, nature, clothing or other objects—not sound. However, pianists have the ability to create a palette of colors on the piano. By using your fingers, wrists and arms in different ways, various sounds and colors can be created through articulation, voicing and dynamics. For example, to achieve a bright color, use strong fingertips. If you want a more muted sound or pastel color, stroke the keys with soft fingertips. To create full, rich colors with chords, you will need to sink into the keys with relaxed wrists and upper arms. As you play, imagine the colors in your music, and then create those colors through your technical approach.

Orchestral Sound

One way to achieve a variety of colors is to think of the piano as an orchestra. As you play, listen to the music and try to imagine which instrument in the orchestra might play that part. Try to imitate the sound of that instrument by experimenting with different ways to use your fingers, wrists and arms.

Listed below are the sections of the orchestra and the instruments found within each section. If you are not familiar with all of these instruments, we recommend that you listen to a recording of Benjamin Britten's *Young Person's Guide to the Orchestra.*

Strings	Woodwinds	Brass	Percussion
Violin	*Piccolo*	*Trumpet*	*Snare drum*
Viola	*Flute*	*French horn*	*Bass drum*
Cello	*Clarinet*	*Trombone*	*Tympani*
Bass	*Oboe*	*Tuba*	*Cymbals*
	Bassoon		*Xylophone*
	Saxophone		*Triangle*

Balance and Voicing

The ability to balance dynamics effectively to bring out the important voice often separates the artistic performer from the average one. Different layers of sound require different dynamics or colors. In general, the melody should be two dynamic levels louder than the accompaniment. For example, if the melody is *mf*, play the accompaniment *p*; if the melody is *mp*, play the accompaniment *pp*. When there are several voices, select even more dynamic levels for effective balance. This ability to create different colors for each voice adds to the character of the music.

It is an even greater challenge when one hand plays two or more notes, and a specific note must be brought out. This is called *voicing*. Many pianists recognize that this ability to bring out the important note (or notes) is one of the most essential elements of good technique. Following are some suggested preparatory exercises to work on voicing.

Voicing Exercises

Exercise 1

- Sink into each half note with a loose wrist and forearm.
- Keep the thumb light and the top note legato.
- Be sure that the top note is *mf* and the bottom note is *pp*.

Exercise 2

- Sink into each half note with a loose wrist and forearm.
- Keep finger 5 light and the bottom note legato.
- Be sure that the bottom note is *mf* and the top note is *pp*.

Exercise 3

- Use a small rocking motion (rotation) to slightly bring out the changing notes (those marked with tenutos).
- In measures 1–3, keep finger 5 light.
- In measures 5–7, keep the thumb light.

Exercise 4

- Sink into each half note in measures 1, 2 and 4, and the quarter notes in measure 3.
- Keep the upper notes soft using a loose, upward wrist motion.
- Be sure that the bass note is louder than the rest of the chord.

While all the "keys" are essential for playing artistically, it is good pedaling that can "make or break" a performance. There are many factors to consider when making pedaling choices, the most important of which is the stylistic period. While some composers have provided pedal markings, in many cases the indicated pedaling might sound incorrect on today's pianos. Some of the factors to consider when making pedaling decisions are: texture, articulation, phrasing, dynamics and color.

By using various lengths and depths of pedal, a variety of colors can be created. Techniques such as *half pedal* and *flutter pedal* are useful for creating certain colors, while avoiding a texture that is too blurred. Sometimes the pedal is used to facilitate legato when the performer is unable to achieve a connected sound with just the fingers.

Good pedal technique requires the correct position of the foot (keeping the ball of the foot on the pedal and heel on the floor). Listen carefully to ensure clear releases of the pedal.

Definitions and Signs

Half pedal—depress the damper pedal halfway.

Flutter pedal—shake your foot quickly up and down on the damper pedal; be sure it is never completely released.

Una corda (u.c.)—depress the soft pedal (left pedal) with your left foot.

Tre corde (t.c.)—release the soft pedal (left pedal); be sure there is no abrupt change in sound.

Syncopated pedaling (Legato pedaling)—depress the damper pedal immediately *after* the first note, then change the pedal with a quick "up-down" motion.

$$\llcorner\underline{\hspace{3cm}}\wedge\underline{\hspace{3cm}}\lrcorner$$

Pedal taps—depress the damper pedal as you play the note, then release the pedal as your finger releases the key.

$$\llcorner\underline{\hspace{1cm}}\lrcorner \quad \llcorner\underline{\hspace{1cm}}\lrcorner \quad \llcorner\underline{\hspace{1cm}}\lrcorner$$

Pedaling Exercises

For all of the exercises below, be sure to keep your heel on the floor and the ball of your foot on the pedal. Always listen carefully for a clear sound as you depress and release the pedal.

Exercise 1: Syncopated Pedaling (Legato Pedaling)

- Depress the damper pedal immediately after the first note.
- As soon as you play the first note in the following measure, quickly release and depress the pedal (with a quick "up-down" motion).
- Count aloud as you play. The pedal goes *up* on beat 1 and *down* on the "&" of beat 1.

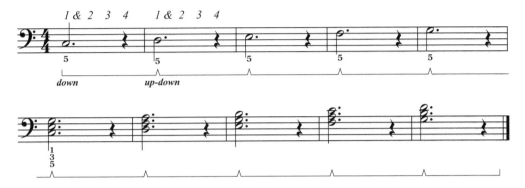

Exercise 2: Syncopated Pedaling (Legato Pedaling)

- Follow the instructions in *Exercise 1* (above).
- Listen carefully to be sure that the harmonies of the previous measure have cleared.

Exercise 3: Pedal Taps

- Depress the damper pedal as you play each note (or chord).
- Release the pedal as your finger releases the key(s).
- Listen carefully to be sure there is no sound during the rests.

Exercise 4: Down-Up Waltz Pedal

- Depress the damper pedal as you play the first note of each measure.
- Keep the pedal down and listen to the sustained sound while your left hand travels to the triad.
- Release the pedal as soon as your left hand plays the triad on beat 2.

Composers usually write pieces with the expectation that the music will be performed with some rhythmic flexibility. The term for rhythmic freedom is *rubato*, which is an Italian word meaning "to rob" or "to steal" (in this case, "stealing" or borrowing time from another beat). *Rubato* should be thought of as the tasteful bending and shaping of the tempo to enhance the musical meaning of the phrase. However, the overall pulse must remain steady.

In some instances, the composer will indicate *rubato*; other times, the performer can decide when to play with more rhythmic freedom, as implied by the music. Some of the places where you might want to play with *rubato* are:

- at the end of a phrase or section of music
- before large melodic leaps or leaps to low bass notes
- at the return of a principal theme

Tempo Terminology

Below are lists of terms that composers often use to indicate the shaping of the tempo.

Terms indicating a slowing of the tempo:

    ritardando—a gradual slowing of the tempo
    rallentando—same as *ritardando*
    ritenuto—immediate slowing of the tempo

Terms indicating a quickening of the tempo:

    accelerando—a gradual increase of the tempo (often over a long passage)
    animato—becoming more lively
    agitato—becoming agitated, excited; moving forward

Special Tempo Symbols

In this book, the editors have provided additional indications for shaping the tempo:

    take a little time (relax the tempo)

    push ahead a little

    breathe (pause)

    take a lot of time (at the end of a section)

Many composers have written pieces with descriptive titles that suggest the mood or character of the music. However, many pieces have non-descriptive titles (such as "Prelude" or "Sonata"). While interpretations may vary, it is important to give the audience a clear idea of the musical message you wish to convey. A good way to do this is to create a story about the music, and assign different moods for each theme.

As you play the pieces in this book, you will notice that some descriptive words are provided. However, you will also see some blank lines on which you should fill in a word that best conveys the mood of the music. Below is a list of expressive words from which to choose. Feel free to add to this list.

agitated	*expressive*	*jolly*	*rippling*
angry	*flowing*	*joyous*	*roaring*
brilliant	*forceful*	*light*	*sad*
calm	*frenzied*	*lively*	*serious*
carefree	*frightening*	*loving*	*shy*
charming	*funny*	*magical*	*simple*
chorale-like	*gentle*	*majestic*	*sneaky*
cute	*ghostly*	*mischievous*	*sparkling*
dancing	*gliding*	*mournful*	*sweet*
delicate	*graceful*	*murmuring*	*stormy*
dramatic	*grand*	*mysterious*	*teasing*
dreamy	*gutsy*	*ominous*	*tender*
drifting	*happy*	*peaceful*	*tragic*
elegant	*heavy*	*pleading*	*triumphant*
energetic	*heroic*	*pompous*	*urgent*
excited	*humorous*	*powerful*	*witty*
explosive	*intimate*	*proud*	*zestful*

Creating Lyrics

Another way to help convey the character of a piece is by creating lyrics that fit the mood of the music. You would not sing these lyrics during a performance, but it is helpful to imagine them as you play. The lyrics you create should match the rhythm and emphasis found in the music. For example, when choosing lyrics for three notes that have an emphasis on the first beat, choose a three-syllable word such as "*beau-ti-ful*" or "*cheer-ful-ly*" (with the accent on the first syllable). Another option is to choose three one-syllable words. Melodies that ascend (go up in pitch) might have lyrics that reflect an upward direction, such as "birds are flying high."

In some of the pieces in this book, lyrics have been provided to help you imagine the character of the piece. Have fun by adding your own lyrics as well.

How a performer moves at the keyboard clearly affects what the audience experiences. More importantly, it affects the way a performer expresses the character of the music and helps the shaping, tone and timing of the piece.

This movement at the keyboard, or choreography, is also helpful in preparing the performer and the audience for the mood of the music. Before you begin playing, lower your head and rest your hands in your lap; this will help you get "into character." When you are about to play, bring your hands to the piano according to the character and tempo of the piece. For example, if you are playing a slow, flowing, elegant piece, you would bring your hands up gracefully.

At the beginning of some pieces in this book, there is a description of an appropriate physical gesture to begin the piece. Also, at the end of some pieces, there is a description of an ending gesture. Throughout the pieces, there are additional directions on how to move your body while playing. All suggestions for choreography are recommended to enhance musical expression and convey the mood of the music.

Choreography Symbols and Terms Used in This Book

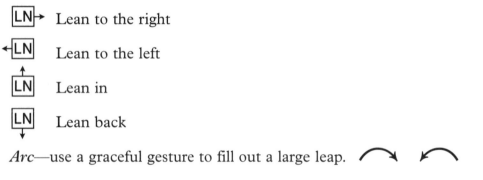

LN→   Lean to the right

←LN   Lean to the left

LN↑   Lean in

LN↓   Lean back

Arc—use a graceful gesture to fill out a large leap.

Freeze—lift the hands over the keyboard and remain still to preserve the character of the music.

Fill out—when holding long notes, keep forearms and elbows moving for the full value of the note.

Place it—a graceful gesture that highlights the importance of a specific note by timing it carefully. Gracefully lift the wrist (∫) and come down with a relaxed wrist.

∫—gracefully lift the wrist at the end of a phrase.

Children's Song

from *For Children,*
Vol. 1, Sz. 42, No. 3

Béla Bartók
(1881–1945)

Keys to this piece:

 Let your body flow and lean with the music to show the shaping of the melody.

 In measures 8, 18 and 22, gracefully lift the wrist at the arrow and carefully "place" the A's for good tone.

Listen for a beautiful melody that projects above the LH accompaniment.

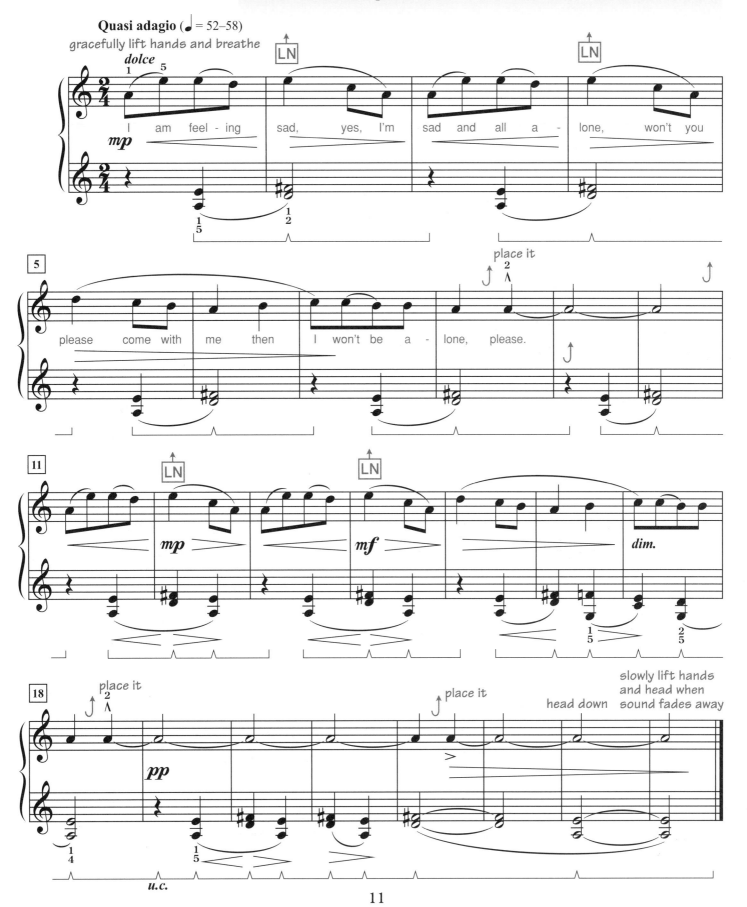

Polka

Michael Ivonovich Glinka
(1804–1857)

 Keys to this piece:

 Let your body move with the music to show the joyful character of this dance.

 Exaggerate the articulation; keep fingertips firm for a crisp staccato.

Listen for a good balance between melody and accompaniment.

Ecossaise in G Major

D. 145, No. 4

Franz Schubert
(1797–1828)

Keys to this piece:

 Bring out the joyful, energetic character of this piece by moving with the music.

 Exaggerate the articulation; keep fingertips firm on staccatos and accents.

 Be sure that the melody always projects above the accompaniment.

(a) Play *f* the first time, and play *mp* on the repeat.

13

Distant Bells

from *12 Melodious Pieces,*
Op. 63, No. 6

J. L. Streabbog
(1835–1886)

 Keys to this piece:

 Make graceful arcs on cross-over gestures during the rests on beat 2, and strike the bell tones on beat 3 with a firm fingertip, relaxed arm and loose wrist.

 Listen for good balance so that the bells always ring clear.

Observe all the pedal indications to create the right colors.

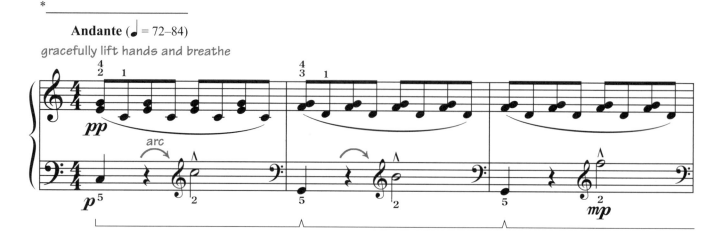

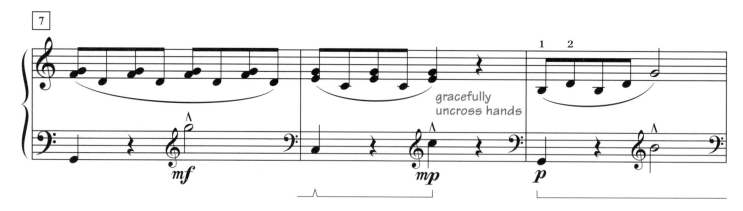

* Write a word on the blank line that conveys the mood of the music (see page 9).

15

Children's Game

from *For Children*,
Vol. 1, Sz. 42, No. 8

Béla Bartók
(1881–1945)

 Keys to this piece:

 Pay careful attention to the composer's very specific articulation. Play on the fingertips for a crisp staccato and listen for a smooth legato where needed.

 Observe all the tempo changes to reflect the piece's changing character.

 In measures with a whole rest, fill out the silence with an arc; make a small arm circle to fill out the half notes in the Adagio section; sit still with head down on fermatas.

* In measures 1, 22, 27, 48 and 53, write a word on the blank line that conveys the mood of the music (see page 9).

16

17

Old French Song

from *Album for the Young,*
Op. 39, No. 16

Peter Ilyich Tchaikovsky
(1840–1893)

Keys to this piece:

Sing the lyrics as you play, letting your voice follow the rise and fall of the melody. Remember to take time at the ends of phrases.

Follow the pedal indications to create a rich, connected sound when legato, and for special color on the staccato notes.

Imagine the piece being played by a string trio (violin, viola, cello).

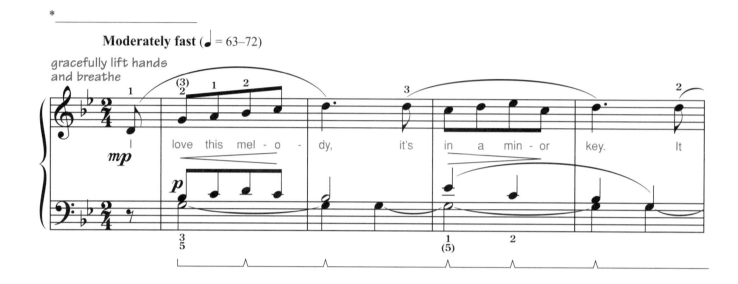

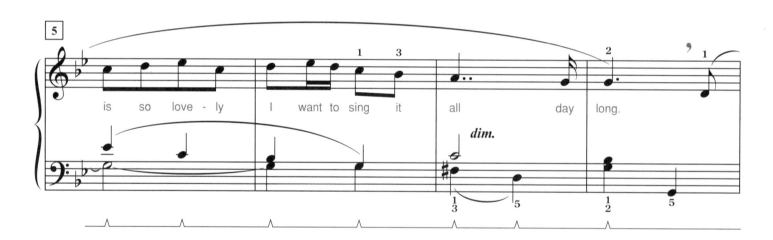

* Write a word on the blank line that conveys the mood of the music (see page 9).

In the Garden

from *Album for the Young,*
Op. 140, No. 4

Cornelius Gurlitt
(1820–1901)

Keys to this piece:

The rich LH melody should sound like a cello and project above the violin-like RH accompaniment; bring out the "duet" in measures 13–16 and 21–31.

Be sure to take time at the ends of phrases.

Listen for clear pedal changes on every bass note.

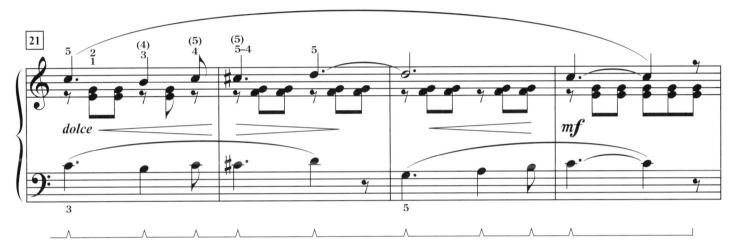

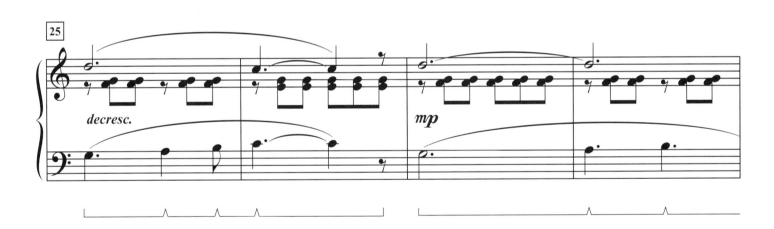

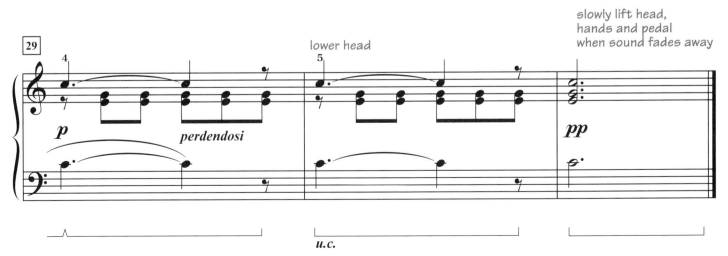

Morning Prayer

from *Album for the Young,*
Op. 39, No. 1

Peter Ilyich Tchaikovsky
(1840–1893)

Keys to this piece:

 Bring out the top note of the RH and slightly bring out the lower note of the LH.

 Use small, sinking motions to create a beautiful tone and calm mood.

Take time at the ends of phrases and lift gently.

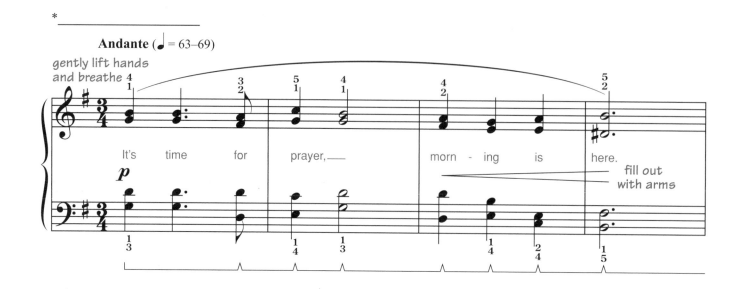

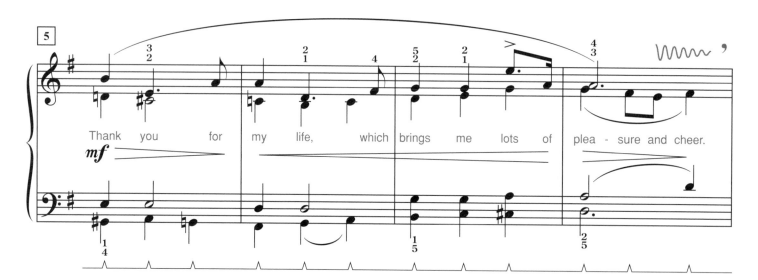

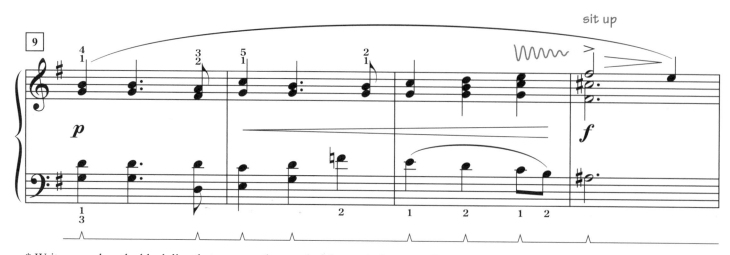

* Write a word on the blank line that conveys the mood of the music (see page 9).

Now bow your head and stay down.

The Festive Dance

from *Album for the Young,*
Op. 140, No. 7

Cornelius Gurlitt
(1820–1901)

 Keys to this piece:

 For a graceful lilt, lift the wrist on all beat-1 quarter notes that are followed by a rest (measures 1 and 3, for example).

 Voice the LH accompaniment by playing the bass note on beat 1 a little louder than beats 2 and 3.

 Use half pedal (1/2) as indicated.

24

A Sad Story

from *12 Melodious Pieces,*
Op. 63, No. 10

J. L. Streabbog
(1835–1886)

Keys to this piece:

Listen for a good balance between melody and accompaniment; keep the repeated chords two dynamic levels softer than the melody.

Observe the pedal markings to help the staccato bass notes ring and the melody notes sing.

Think of a sad story and add your own lyrics.

Italian Song

from *Album for the Young,*
Op. 39, No. 15

Peter Ilyich Tchaikovsky
(1840–1893)

Keys to this piece:

Gracefully lift the wrist at the ends of phrases.

For a good balance, play the melody one dynamic level louder than the bass note (beat 1), and two levels louder on beats 2 and 3.

Bring out the joyful, dance-like character by singing the lyrics and letting your body flow with the music.

28

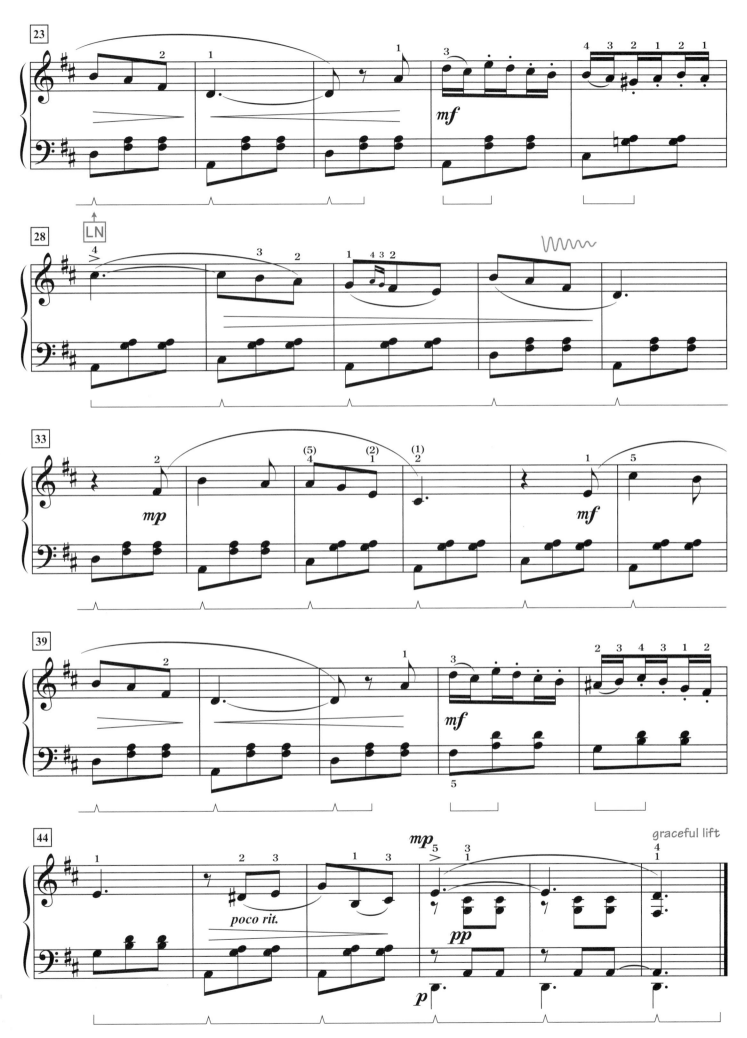

Peasant Dance

Op. 107, No. 20

Carl Reinecke
(1824–1910)

Keys to this piece:

Reflect the joyful dance character by letting your body move with the music.

To create a bright color on all the staccatos, accents and slurs, use firm fingertips and loose wrists.

Imagine an orchestra playing this piece; write the names of different instruments for various sections of the music.

* Write a word on the blank line that conveys the mood of the music (see page 9).

First Loss

from *Album for the Young*,
Op. 68, No. 16

Robert Schumann
(1810–1856)

Keys to this piece:

 Lift the hands gracefully at the ends of phrases.

 Use an arc motion for leaps (measures 8, 16, etc.).

 To get into the character of the music, think of someone or something that, if lost, would make you sad (then fill in the blanks in measures 5–6).

I'm real-ly ver-y sad, oh, yes I am, I've

lost my _____, where can _____ be? I'm sad and blue.

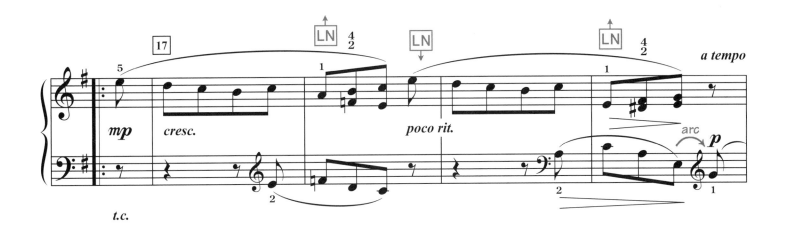

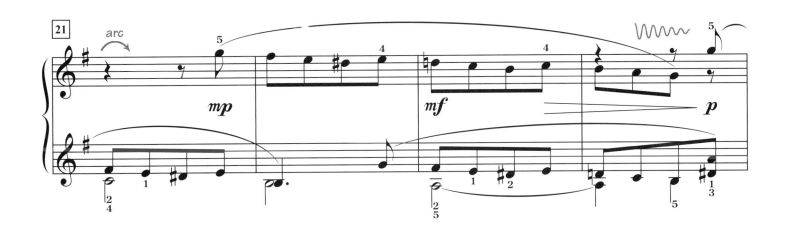

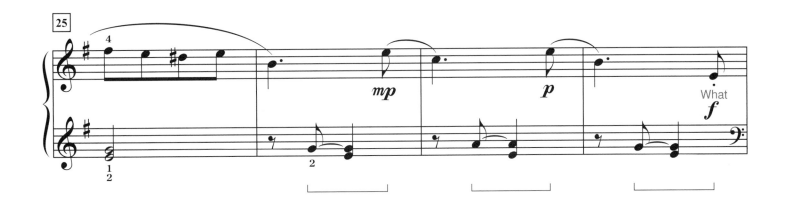

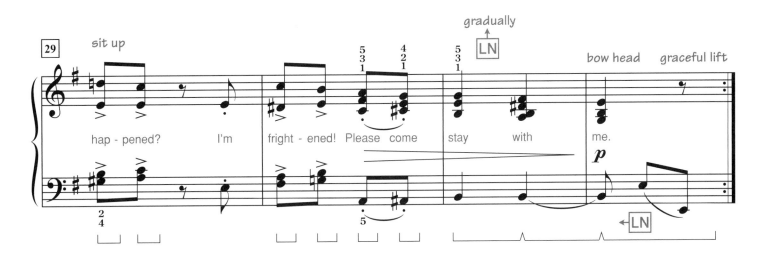

33

Waltz

Op. 36, No. 3

Amy Beach
(1867–1944)

Ländler

D. 679, No. 2

Franz Schubert
(1797–1828)

Keys to this piece:

 Experience the dance-like character of the piece by moving gracefully with the music.

 Listen for a good balance between the RH melody and LH accompaniment.

 Observe the pedal markings to bring out the lilting character of the music.

with hands on the piano, hear
measures 7–8 as an Intro

Allegretto (♩ = 138–152)

Watch me turn a-round, oh, yes I turn a-round, and now I'm stand-ing tall so proud - ly.

Stand up tall then bow.

sit up

Turn a-round, and then we slow down now, and bow your head.

poco rit.

graceful lift

LN

ⓐ Play *mf* the first time, and play *p* on the repeat.

37

Waltz in B Minor

Op. 18, D. 145, No. 6

Franz Schubert
(1791–1828)

Keys to this piece:

Lean your body in the direction of the melody.

Slow down at the ends of phrases, especially at the change to B major (measure 25).

For a good balance, play the melody one dynamic level louder than the bass note and two levels louder than the chords.

stand up tall, high on your toes, then gent - ly tap your toes and lean in close.

ped. simile

u.c.　　　　　　　　　　　　　　　　　　　*t.c.*

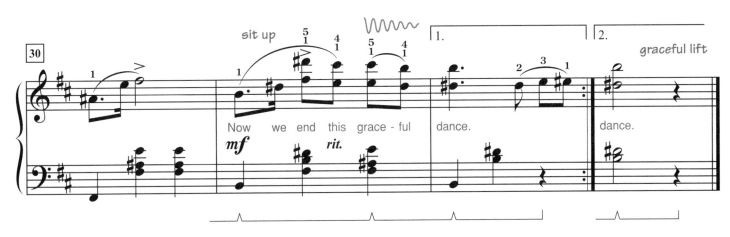

Now we end this grace - ful dance.　　dance.

March Breve

Dennis Alexander
(b. 1947)

 Keys to this piece:

 Listen for a good dynamic balance; the LH should sound like a soft drum beat.

 Exaggerate the articulation; keep fingertips firm for a crisp staccato; listen for a smooth legato when indicated.

Imagine soldiers marching as you keep a steady tempo and a strict dotted rhythm.

40

Siciliana

from *11 Children's Pieces,*
Op. 35, No. 6

Alfredo Casella
(1883–1947)

Keys to this piece:

Imagine an oboe playing the RH melody, with a soft string accompaniment in the LH.

Slow down to bring out the interesting harmonic changes in measures 12-13 and 31-32.

Listen for clear pedal changes.

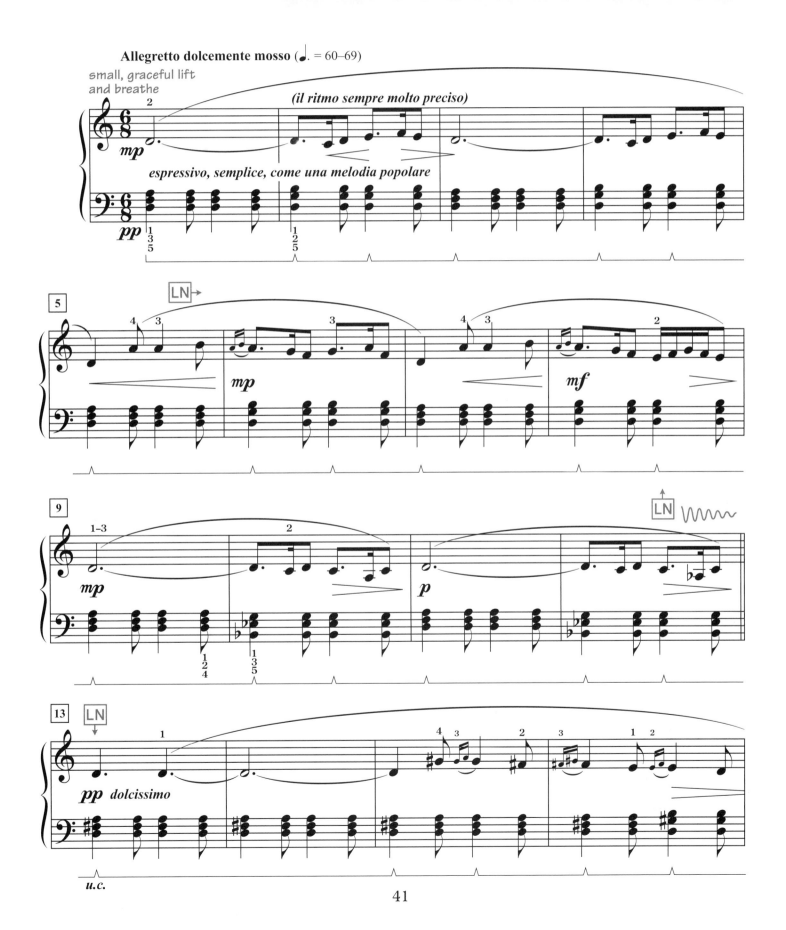

Butterflies

from *12 Melodious Pieces,*
Op. 63, No. 11

J. L. Streabogg
(1835–1886)

Keys to this piece:

 Be sure that the RH melody always projects above the LH accompaniment.

 Use small, graceful "down-up" wrist gestures on all the slurs; keep fingertips firm for a clean sound.

 Sing the lyrics (and add your own) to capture the character of the butterflies flying around.

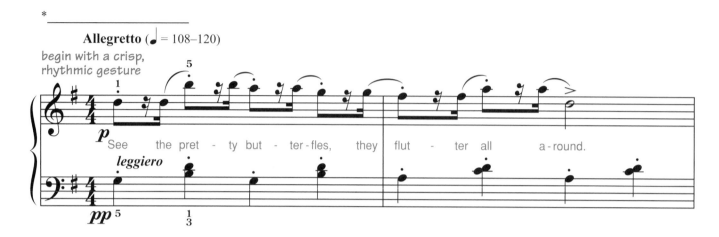

Allegretto (♩ = 108–120)

begin with a crisp, rhythmic gesture

p leggiero *pp*

See the pret - ty but - ter - fles, they flut - ter all a - round.

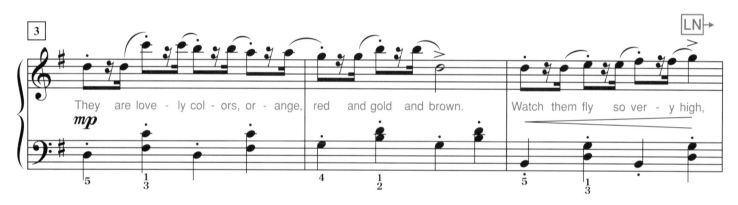

They are love - ly col - ors, or - ange, red and gold and brown. Watch them fly so ver - y high,

mp

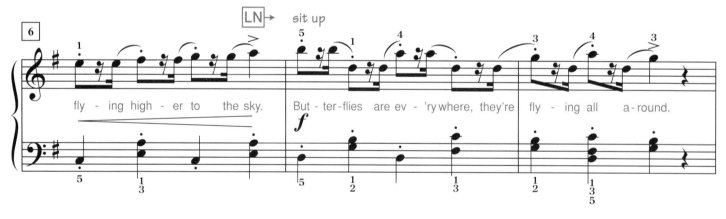

fly - ing high - er to the sky. But - ter - flies are ev - 'ry where, they're fly - ing all a - round.

f

add your own lyrics

* Write a word on the blank line that conveys the mood of the music (see page 9).

44

Elizabeth's Lullaby

*for Elizabeth Faith Newell
and her family*

Dennis Alexander
(b. 1947)

Keys to this piece:

 Sing the melody as you play, remembering to breathe at the ends of phrases; imagine a grandmother singing to her granddaughter.

 Keep the LH soft and flowing, lifting gracefully on the rests; slightly bring out the changing bass notes on the first beat in measures 5-7, 12-15 and 29-32.

Let your body flow gracefully to reflect the calm mood.

Lull - a - by   and good - night,   go   to   sleep.   *rit.*

keep head down until
sound fades away

p   arc

place it

47

Toccata Robusto

Dennis Alexander
(b. 1947)

 Keys to this piece:

 Listen for a clear contrast between legato and staccato touches.

 Bring out the robust character by exaggerating the crisp gestures of the alternating hands (the gestures should get bigger as you get louder).

 Move your arms with dramatic arcs when playing large leaps (measures 33-35, 45-52).

Allegro e molto ritmico ($\quad$ = 108–120)

begin with a crisp, rhythmic gesture

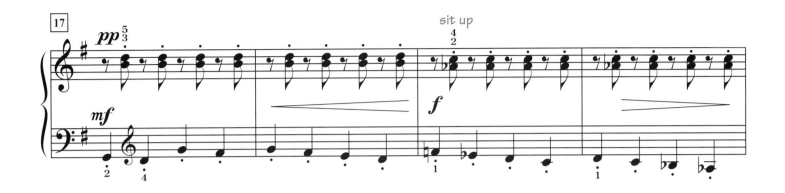

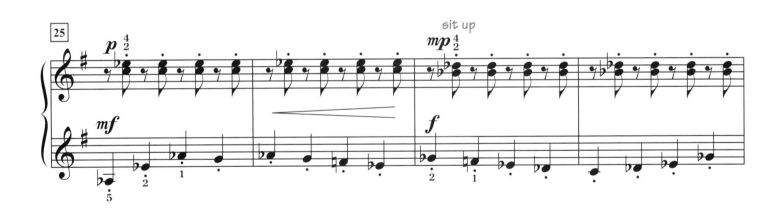

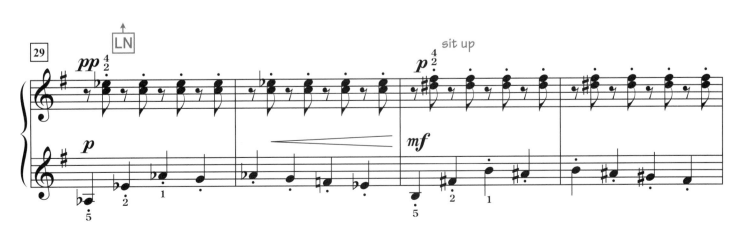

The Mysterious Nile

Dennis Alexander
(b. 1947)

Keys to this piece:

Project and shape the expressive RH melody above a softer LH accompaniment.

Let your body flow gently with the music, leaning slightly in the direction of the melody; move your arms with graceful arcs when there are large leaps.

Create a mysterious color by imagining an oboe playing the melody and strings playing the accompaniment.

51

Murmuring Brook

from *Album for the Young*,
Op. 140, No 5

Cornelius Gurlitt
(1820–1901)

Keys to this piece:

Be sure to bring out the melody (double-stemmed notes).

Sing the melody as you play, following the rise and fall of the line; remember to breathe at the ends of phrases.

Use half pedal on every eighth note to achieve the correct color.

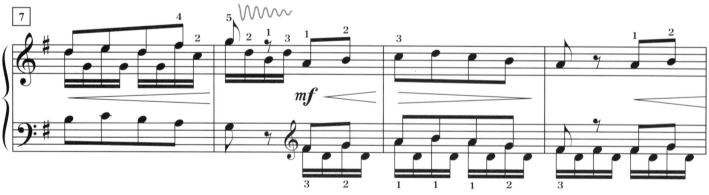

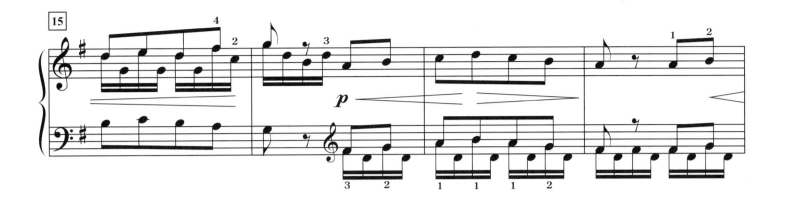

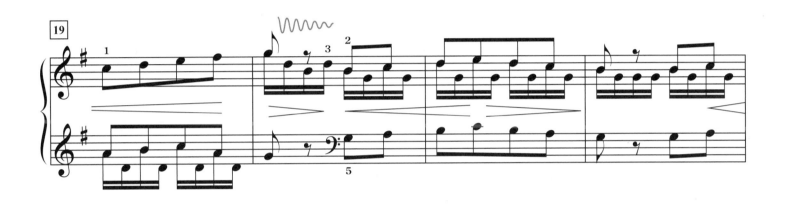

keep head down until
sound fades away,
then slowly lift

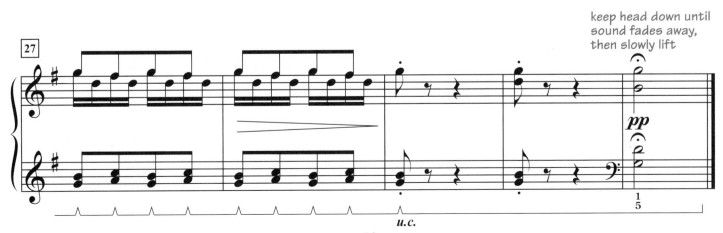

u.c.

53

Scherzino

Dennis Alexander
(b. 1947)

Keys to this piece:

Pay careful attention to the composer's very specific articulation; play on the fingertips for a crisp staccato and listen for a smooth legato when needed.

Let your body dance with the music to bring out the playful character of the piece.

Listen for a good balance between the hands; the accompaniment should be two dynamic levels softer than the melody.

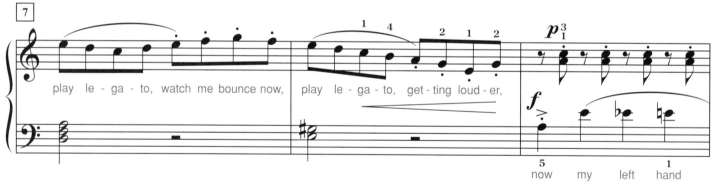

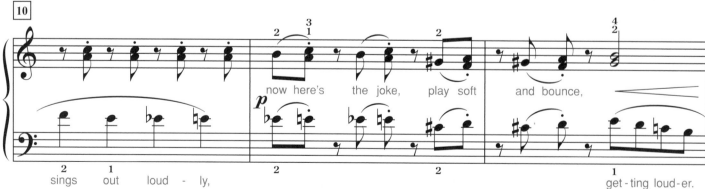

* Write a word on the blank line that conveys the mood of the music (see page 9).

Ingrid Jacobson Clarfield

Ingrid Jacobson Clarfield is a Professor of Piano and Coordinator of the Piano Department at Westminster Choir College of Rider University. She is an active performer, author, and clinician, and has presented pedagogy workshops, master classes, and lecture-recitals in over 100 cities throughout the U.S. and Canada. Her students have won numerous awards at state, national and international competitions. She has performed in two-piano recitals with Lillian Livingston since 1976. Ms. Clarfield is a co-author of *Keys to Stylistic Mastery,* and the author of *Burgmüller, Czerny, Hanon: Piano Studies Selected for Technique and Musicality.* Her editions of Debussy's *Golliwog's Cakewalk,* Beethoven's *Moonlight Sonata* and Chopin's *Nocturne in E-flat Major, Op. 9, No. 2,* are part of her *Artistic Preparation and Performance Series* (Alfred Publishing Co.). Her articles have been published in *American Music Teacher, Keyboard Companion, Piano Life* and *Clavier.* Ms. Clarfield received her B.M. at Oberlin College where she studied with John Perry, and an M.M. from the Eastman School of Music. In 2006, Ms. Clarfield was honored to be selected as an MTNA Foundation Fellow.

Dennis Alexander

Since his affiliation with Alfred Publishing Company in 1986 as a composer and clinician, Dennis Alexander has earned an international reputation as one of North America's most prolific and popular composers of educational piano music for students at all levels. Professor Alexander retired from his position at the University of Montana in May 1996 where he taught piano and piano pedagogy for 24 years. He currently resides in Albuquerque, New Mexico, where he teaches privately while maintaining an active composing and touring schedule for Alfred Publishing Company.

Over the years, numerous organizations and state associations have commissioned him to write compositions. Many of his compositions are included in the National Federation of Music Study Clubs Festival required list, and his music is being performed by students throughout the United States, Canada, South Africa, Australia, Asia and Europe. Mr. Alexander is also a co-author of *Alfred's Premier Piano Course.*